CREATIVE COOKING COLLECTION

Entertaining

CREATIVE COOKING COLLECTION

Entertaining

Roz Denny

CONTENTS

Published exclusively for Cupress (Canada) Limited
10 Falconer Drive, Unit 8, Mississauga,
Ontario L5N 1B1, Canada
by Woodhead-Faulkner Ltd

First published 1987
© Woodhead-Faulkner (Publishers) Ltd 1987
All rights reserved
ISBN 0-920691-17-X
Printed and bound in Singapore

INTRODUCTION

Entertaining can be fun for some—and nerve-wracking for others! There are those who like to spend a long time preparing a meal, paying great attention to detail—while others prefer the quicker more casual approach.

For novice entertainers, I strongly advise learning the art of entertaining gradually—start with just two guests and a simple meal, then increase your guest list and repertoire as your skill improves.

Organization is essential if you wish to spend most of your time with your guests. Prepare vegetables, salads and garnishes beforehand, storing them in the refrigerator to cook or serve at the last minute. Set the table and get the glasses and nibbles ready for aperitifs early in the day, then you can concentrate on the food. But don't be embarrassed to disappear into the kitchen occasionally for short periods—it shows that you are preparing freshly cooked food.

MENU PLANNING

Food should not go unnoticed—it should please the eye as well as the palate. The menus in this book have been planned to complement each other in style and content: light followed by fuller flavour, creaminess followed by sharpness and crunch, and so on. If you would prefer to mix and match the dishes, try and balance the flavours, textures and colours.

As rich desserts are becoming less popular, I have included a few savouries —an old, very British idea regaining favour. Serve them after or instead of the dessert, followed by fruit, and cheese if you wish.

WINES AND DRINKS

Choosing a wine is personal and the suggestions are intended to be guides only. In some cases I have simply given one or two wines if the menu is more casual. Sometimes it is a nice idea to start with a dry sherry or white port, or even drink a flower or herb tea throughout the meal.

Do be careful not to ply your guests with too much alcohol. Many will have to drive home, so it is a good idea to have bottles of mineral water as well.

NOTES

Ingredients are given in both metric and imperial measures. Use either set of quantities but not a mixture of both in any one recipe.

All spoon measurements are level:
1 tablespoon = one 15 ml spoon
1 teaspoon = one 5 ml spoon.

Ovens should be preheated to the temperature specified.

Freshly ground black pepper is intended where pepper is listed.

Fresh herbs are used unless otherwise stated. If unobtainable dried herbs can be substituted in cooked dishes but halve the quantities.

Eggs are large size unless otherwise stated.

SEASONAL MENUS

This collection of four menus is based on the seasons, taking into account the availability of fresh foods and the type of meal that suits the weather—e.g. light in summer, warming in winter. Of course, with the wide range of imported ingredients and frozen foods now available, many of the dishes could be prepared all year round.

SPRING MENU FOR SIX
Sole and Asparagus Rolls, Celebration Roast Lamb, Tuiles Fruit Baskets.
Suggested Wines. *Starter:* Piesporter Michelsberg, or a Chablis. *Main Course:* Chianti Classico Riserva, or Beaujolais. *Dessert:* Muscat de Beaumes de Venise.

SUMMER MENU FOR FOUR
Watercress Stuffed Tomatoes, Salmon and Ginger Steaks, Summer Ramekins.
Suggested Wines. *Starter and Main Course:* Alsace Pinot Blanc, or white Burgundy. *Dessert:* Vouvray Château des Bidaudières.

AUTUMN MENU FOR FOUR
Zucchini and Chèvre Soufflés, Duck Breasts with Lemon Sauce, Fruit Shells.
Suggested Wines. *Starter:* Orvieto Secco. *Main Course:* Beaujolais, or St. Emilion.

WINTER MENU FOR SIX
Mussel and Saffron Soup, Spiced Beef with Almond Prunes, Georgian Jellies.
Suggested Wines. *Starter:* Muscadet de Sèvre et Maine. *Main Course:* Médoc.

WATERCRESS STUFFED TOMATOES

4 large tomatoes
1 bunch watercress
125 g (4 oz) cottage cheese, or soft goat's cheese
2 green onions, chopped finely
1 teaspoon horseradish cream or relish
few curly endive or frisé leaves
6–8 tablespoons vinaigrette dressing
salt and pepper to taste

Serves 4
Preparation time: 25 minutes
Freezing: Not recommended

Illustrated below right: Zucchini and Chèvre Soufflés (page 10)

1. Cut the rounded ends off the tomatoes, scoop out the flesh and discard with the ends (or use for another dish).
2. Remove the stalks from half of the watercress and chop the leaves finely. Mix into the cheese with the green onions, horseradish, and salt and pepper. Pile into the tomato shells.
3. Place the remaining watercress and the curly endive in a bowl. Toss in half of the vinaigrette dressing.
4. Place the tomatoes on individual serving plates, trickle over the remaining vinaigrette dressing and garnish with the salad. Serve chilled.

SOLE AND ASPARAGUS ROLLS

3 soles, skinned and
   filleted (bones and heads
   reserved)
225 ml (1 cup) dry white
   wine
1 onion, sliced
1 carrot, sliced
bouquet garni of bayleaf,
   parsley and thyme

450 ml (1¾ cups) water
12 asparagus spears
juice of ½ lemon
3 egg yolks
salt and pepper to taste
TO GARNISH:
125 g (4 oz) small button
   mushrooms, cooked
   lightly in boiling water

Serves 6
Preparation time:
45 minutes
Cooking time:
15–20 minutes
Freezing:
Not recommended

1. Place the fish bones and heads, wine, onion, carrot, bouquet garni, water, and salt and pepper in a pan and simmer for 20 minutes. Strain and reserve the stock.
2. Cut the asparagus about 10 cm (4 inches) from the tips. Place the stalks and reserved fish stock in a pan, cover and cook gently for 15 minutes, until quite soft; add the tips for the last 5 minutes. Drain, reserving the stock, and keep warm.
3. Season the fish with salt and pepper and sprinkle with the lemon juice. Fold the asparagus stalks in half, place on the fish and roll up. Place join side down in a shallow ovenproof dish.
4. Pour over the reserved stock, season with salt and pepper, cover and cook in a preheated oven, 190°C/375°F, for 15–20 minutes, until tender. Transfer to a warmed serving dish with a slotted spoon and keep warm.
5. Strain 300 ml (1¼ cups) of the reserved stock into a saucepan and boil hard until reduced by half.
6. Place the egg yolks, and salt and pepper in a bowl over a pan of simmering water and whisk to a stiff foam. Stir in the reduced stock until creamy.
7. Spoon over the sole rolls and garnish with the asparagus tips and mushrooms to serve.

MUSSEL AND SAFFRON SOUP

large pinch of saffron
   strands
4 kg (8 lb) mussels in shells
600 ml (2½ cups) fish
   stock or water
2 tablespoons butter
2 large onions, chopped
2 cloves garlic, crushed

150 ml (⅔ cup) dry white
   wine
½ cup whole wheat flour
600 ml (2½ cups) milk
4 tablespoons chopped
   parsley
salt and pepper to taste

1. Soak the saffron strands in 3 tablespoons boiling water for 15 minutes.

2. Discard any mussels that are open. Scrub the rest and place in a large saucepan. Add the stock or water, cover and simmer for about 5 minutes, until the shells open; discard any that do not open. Drain, reserving the liquor.

3. Scrape the mussels from the shells and set aside; reserve a few empty shells for garnishing.

4. Melt the butter in a pan, add the onion and garlic and fry gently for 3 minutes. Add the wine and cook, uncovered, until reduced by half.

5. Stir in the flour and cook for 2 minutes, then add the milk and reserved mussel liquor. Bring to the boil, stirring, then add the saffron and its soaking water. Season well with salt and pepper and simmer for 5 minutes.

6. Add the parsley and mussels and heat through gently; do not allow to boil or the mussels will toughen.

7. Replace a mussel in each of the reserved shells and float on the soup to serve.

Serves 6
Preparation time:
40 minutes
Cooking time:
15 minutes
Freezing:
Not recommended

ZUCCHINI AND CHÈVRE SOUFFLÉS

These individual soufflés can be prepared about an hour ahead and then cooked while your guests are having drinks, but they must be served straight from the oven.

2 tablespoons butter	4 tablespoons milk
3 zucchini, chopped finely	2 eggs, separated
1 small onion, chopped	2 tablespoons freshly grated Parmesan cheese
1 clove garlic, crushed	2 tablespoons dried breadcrumbs
1/3 cup flour	1 1/2 tablespoons slivered almonds
50 g (2 oz) soft goat's cheese, derinded and chopped	salt and pepper to taste

Serves 4
Preparation time: 20 minutes
Cooking time: About 25 minutes
Freezing: Recommended at end of stage 4. Part thaw and cook for 30 minutes.

Illustrated on page 7

1. Melt the butter in a pan, add the zucchini, onion, garlic and 1 tablespoon water and sauté gently for 5 minutes, until pulpy. Stir in the flour and simmer for 1 minute.
2. Add the cheese, milk, egg yolks, Parmesan, and salt and pepper, stirring well.
3. Whisk the egg whites until stiff, then fold in gently.
4. Lightly grease 4 individual soufflé dishes and coat with the breadcrumbs. Divide the mixture between the dishes and sprinkle with the almonds.
5. Bake in a preheated oven, 190°C/375°F, for about 25 minutes, until well risen. Serve immediately.

CELEBRATION ROAST LAMB

If using a saddle of lamb, brush the kidneys with oil and cover with foil before cooking. If serving a crown roast, fill the centre with a selection of crisp vegetables to serve.

saddle, large crown roast or leg of lamb, weighing 2.25 kg (5 lb)	6 tablespoons red wine vinegar
2 cloves garlic, sliced	bouquet garni of bayleaf, thyme and parsley
2 rosemary sprigs	2 tablespoons corn starch, blended with 1 tablespoon water
600 ml (2 1/2 cups) lamb stock	4 tablespoons ginger wine
1 tablespoon oil	2 tablespoons redcurrant jelly
2 shallots or 1 onion, chopped	rosemary sprigs to garnish
1 carrot, chopped	

1. Stab the lamb in several places with a sharp pointed knife and place the garlic and rosemary in each cut. Weigh the joint, allowing 20–25 minutes per 500 g (1 lb), depending on how well done you like your meat, and cook in a preheated oven, 180°C/350°F, for the calculated time. Place the lamb on a serving dish and keep warm. Drain off the fat from the pan.

2. Pour the stock into the pan and scrape up all the meaty residue. Reserve.

3. Heat the oil in a pan, add the shallots, or onion, and carrot and sauté for 10 minutes. Add the vinegar and boil until it evaporates.

4. Add the reserved stock and bouquet garni and simmer for 5 minutes. Stir in the blended corn starch, then add the ginger wine and redcurrant jelly and simmer for 3 minutes. Strain into a sauce boat.

5. Garnish the lamb with rosemary sprigs and serve with Potatoes Boulangère (page 77), a vegetable purée, such as carrot (see page 79) and a green vegetable. Hand the sauce separately.

Serves 6
Preparation time:
15 minutes
Cooking time:
1½–2 hours
Freezing:
Not recommended

DUCK BREASTS WITH LEMON SAUCE

*4 duck breasts, each
weighing 175 g (6 oz),
skinned
whole wheat flour for
coating
1 tablespoon olive oil
1 tablespoon butter*

*1 large clove garlic, sliced
juice of 1 lemon
2 teaspoons sugar
salt and pepper to taste
lemon twists to garnish*

Serves 4
Preparation time:
10 minutes
Cooking time:
10–15 minutes
Freezing:
Not recommended

1. Toss the duck breasts in flour to coat evenly.
2. Heat the oil and butter gently in a pan, add the garlic and fry slowly until it starts to brown; discard.
3. Increase the heat and add the duck breasts. Fry for about 5 minutes on each side or until cooked to your liking.
4. Pour in the lemon juice, sprinkle with the sugar and season with salt and pepper.
5. Slice the breasts diagonally and garnish with twists of lemon. Serve with Baby Rösti (page 78) and Peas with Lettuce (page 76).

SALMON AND GINGER STEAKS

*4 salmon steaks, each
weighing 250 g (8 oz)
¼ cup butter, softened
2 teaspoons grated fresh
root ginger
75 g (3 oz) fennel, sliced
thinly*

*75 g (3 oz) each carrot
and leek, cut into
julienne strips
2–3 tablespoons dry
sherry (optional)
salt and pepper to taste*

Serves 4
Preparation time:
15 minutes
Cooking time:
20–25 minutes
Freezing:
Not recommended

1. Place the salmon steaks in a shallow ovenproof dish and season with salt and pepper.
2. Mix the butter with the ginger and spread half on the salmon steaks.
3. Blanch the vegetables in boiling water for 2 minutes. Drain and place on the salmon.
4. Sprinkle with the sherry, if using, and top with the remaining butter. Season lightly with salt and pepper.
5. Cover and cook in a preheated oven, 190°C/375°F, for 20–25 minutes or until cooked.
6. Serve with new potatoes, Green Beans in Tomato Concasse (page 76) and a crisp salad.

SPICED BEEF WITH ALMOND PRUNES

6 slices braising beef, each
  weighing 175 g (6 oz)
  and about 2 cm
  (3/4 inch) thick
2 onions, sliced
2 carrots, sliced
2 cloves garlic, crushed
1 teaspoon ground
  coriander
1/2 teaspoon ground cloves
300 ml (1 1/4 cups) red wine
3 tablespoons brandy
  (optional)
2 tablespoons olive oil
175 g (6 oz) bacon, diced

2 tablespoons whole wheat
  flour
450 ml (1 3/4 cups) strong
  beef stock
large bouquet garni of
  bayleaf, parsley and
  thyme
3 thin strips orange rind
12 large pitted prunes
12 whole almonds
salt and pepper to taste
FOR THE FLEURONS:
1/2 × 250 g (8.8 oz) packet
  puff pastry
beaten egg to glaze

Serves 6
Preparation time:
25 minutes, plus
marinating
Cooking time:
2¼ hours
Freezing:
Recommended

1. Place the beef, onions, carrots, garlic and spices in a large dish, pour over the wine and brandy, if using, and leave to marinate overnight.
2. Drain, reserving the marinade.
3. Heat the oil in a pan, add the beef and fry quickly on both sides to brown. Remove and set aside.
4. Add the marinated vegetables and the bacon to the pan and sauté for about 5 minutes.
5. Add the flour and cook, stirring, for 2 minutes. Add the reserved marinade and the stock, bring to the boil and cook for 2 minutes.
6. Transfer to a casserole and add the meat, herbs, orange rind, and salt and pepper. Cover and cook in a preheated oven, 170°C/325°F, for about 2 hours or until tender.
7. Stuff the prunes with the almonds and add to the casserole for the last 20 minutes of cooking.
8. To make the fleurons, roll out the pastry to a ¼ inch thickness. Using a fluted 5 cm (2 inch) cutter, stamp out half moon shapes. Brush with beaten egg. Increase the oven temperature to 200°C/400°F and bake for 10–15 minutes, until golden. Scatter on top of the casserole.
9. Serve with baked potatoes, Creamed Sprouts (page 77) and crisply cooked seasonal vegetables.

SUMMER RAMEKINS

1 passion fruit
500 g (1 lb) mixed soft
    fruit, e.g. strawberries,
    raspberries, cherries
4 tablespoons liquid honey
2 tablespoons water

8 small slices whole wheat
    bread
TO SERVE:
1–2 tablespoons table
    cream
mint leaves to decorate

Serves 4
Preparation time:
20 minutes, plus
chilling
Cooking time:
5 minutes
Freezing:
Recommended

1. Cut the passion fruit in half and scoop out the pulp.
2. Place the passion fruit pulp and prepared soft fruit in a pan, add the honey and water and cook for about 5 minutes, until the juice runs. Leave to cool.
3. Lightly grease 4 individual ramekins and line the bases with foil or waxed paper.
4. Cut out 8 rounds of bread the size of the ramekins and put one in each dish.
5. Spoon on the fruit, draining slightly; there should be about 200 ml (¾ cup) juice remaining. Rub this through a sieve and set aside.
6. Top the fruit in the ramekins with the remaining bread, weigh down lightly with cups and chill overnight.
7. Turn out onto individual plates and spoon over the reserved juice, thinned with a little water if necessary.
8. Dip a skewer into the cream, then swirl into the sauce around each pudding. Decorate with mint to serve.

TUILES FRUIT BASKETS

The tuiles can be made in advance and stored in an airtight container. Prepare the fruit sauces ahead, but spoon in the prepared fruits just before serving.

FOR THE TUILES:
3 egg whites
½ cup sugar
¾ cup flour, sifted
2 tablespoons butter,
    melted
grated rind of 1 orange
FOR THE GOOSEBERRY
    AND KIWI SAUCE:
500 g (1 lb) gooseberries
4 tablespoons liquid
    honey
2 kiwi fruit, peeled

½ cup cottage cheese
FOR THE RASPBERRY
    COULIS:
250 g (8 oz) raspberries
2 tablespoons icing sugar
TO SERVE:
500 g (1 lb) mixed soft
    fruit, e.g. strawberries,
    raspberries, peaches,
    plums, apricots
icing sugar for sprinkling

1. Beat the ingredients for the tuiles together until smooth.

2. Place dessertspoons of the mixture well apart on well greased baking sheets, 2 per sheet, and bake in a pre-heated oven, 180°C/350°F, for 10 minutes.

3. Scoop off immediately with a palette knife and place over an orange or upturned cup. Press down lightly to mould, then place on a wire rack to cool.

4. Place the gooseberries and honey in a pan and cook for about 10 minutes, until pulpy.

5. Cool slightly, then place in a blender or food processor with the kiwi fruit and cheese and work until smooth. Rub through a sieve.

6. Purée the raspberries and icing sugar in a blender or food processor, then rub through a sieve. Chill both sauces until required.

7. Fill each tuile with mixed summer fruits and dust lightly with icing sugar. Place on individual serving plates, with a pool of each sauce.

Serves 6 (but the mixture makes extra baskets)
Preparation time: 30 minutes
Cooking time: 30 minutes
Freezing: Not recommended

FRAGRANT FRUIT SHELLS

1 pineapple, halved
1 paw paw or mango,
    peeled and sliced
1 kiwi fruit, peeled, halved
    and sliced

2 teaspoons orange flower
    water
250 g (8 oz) strawberries,
    sliced
1 tablespoon icing sugar

Serves 4
Preparation time:
15 minutes
Freezing:
Not recommended

1. Cut the pineapple flesh from the shells, leaving the shells intact.
2. Mix the pineapple, paw paw or mango, kiwi fruit and orange flower water together with a third of the strawberries. Pile back into the pineapple shells.
3. Purée the remaining strawberries with the icing sugar in a blender or food processor.
4. Trickle a little of the strawberry purée over the fruit. Serve the remainder separately.

GEORGIAN JELLIES

150 ml (2/3 cup) freshly
    squeezed lemon juice,
    strained (juice of about
    4 lemons)
3 tablespoons medium
    sherry
4 strips lemon rind
3 tablespoons sugar
6 teaspoons gelatine

450 ml (1¾ cups) freshly
    squeezed orange juice,
    strained (juice of about
    4 large oranges)
4 strips orange rind
6 tablespoons table cream
    (optional)
mint leaves to decorate

Serves 6
Preparation time:
20 minutes, plus
setting time
Cooking time:
6 minutes
Freezing:
Not recommended

1. Make the lemon juice and sherry up to 600 ml (2½ cups) with boiling water. Place in a pan, add the lemon rind and sugar, then simmer for 3 minutes. Remove from the heat.
2. Sprinkle in half of the gelatine, stirring briskly until dissolved. Leave to cool.
3. Strain into 6 wine glasses and chill until set; about 4 hours.
4. Place the orange juice and rind in a pan, bring to the boil, then simmer for 3 minutes. Add sugar to taste, if required. Sprinkle in the remaining gelatine, stirring until dissolved. Leave to cool, then strain.
5. When the lemon layer has set, pour over the orange jelly and leave to set.
6. If wished, pour 1 tablespoon table cream over each jelly before serving. Decorate with mint and serve accompanied by dessert biscuits.

ANYTIME MENUS

MENU FOR SIX
Leek, Tomato and Cheese Salad, Ella's Roast Pork, Choux Buns with Mango Cream.
Suggested wines. *Starter:* Chilled white port or dry sherry if you wish. *Main course:* Portuguese rosé, or a white Dão, or Californian Zinfandel.

MENU FOR FOUR
Pasta with Tomato Sauce and Zucchini, Haddock and Whiting Turban, Coffee and Walnut Roulade.
Suggested wines. *Starter:* Anjou Rouge. *Main course:* Burgundy, Chardonnay.

MENU FOR FOUR
Avocado with Two Caviars, Lamb with Watercress in Filo, Apples with Sauternes Sauce.
Suggested wines. *Starter:* Alsace Sylvaner. *Main course:* any Beaujolais. *Dessert:* the rest of the Sauternes.

MENU FOR FOUR
Warm Spinach Salad, Guinea Fowl with Cucumber, Brandied Bread Pudding.
Suggested wines. *Starter:* Muscadet de Sèvre et Maine. *Main course:* Domaine du Colombier Chinon, or Cabernet Franc D'Aquilea.

MENU FOR FOUR
Caesar Salad, Pork Dijonnaise, Apricot Amaretti Fool.
Suggested wine. *Main course:* Rioja, Vino Alberdi, or Coteaux du Tricastin.

AVOCADO WITH TWO CAVIARS

2 large ripe avocados, peeled, halved and stoned
FOR THE DRESSING:
2/3 cup sour cream
1 tablespoon wine vinegar
2 tablespoons sunflower oil
1/2 teaspoon mustard powder
1 teaspoon fine sugar
salt and pepper to taste
TO SERVE:
25 g (1 oz) each red and black lumpfish roe caviar
snipped chives (optional)

Serves 4
Preparation time: 10 minutes
Freezing: Not recommended

1. Slash the avocado halves from the wide base almost to the top and fan out on 4 serving plates.
2. Whisk the dressing ingredients together. Pour some around the avocados; serve the rest separately.
3. Garnish with alternate mounds of caviar and sprinkle the dressing with chives if you wish. Serve immediately.

CAESAR SALAD

In America in the 1920s, one Caesar Cardini devised a salad based on simple ingredients—bread, lettuce, Parmesan cheese, eggs and the best olive oil. It became very popular with the Hollywood movie world and is now a culinary legend.

3 cloves garlic
5 tablespoons virgin olive oil
4 slices whole grain bread, crusts removed, diced
1 Romaine lettuce
50 g (2 oz) Parmesan cheese, grated

FOR THE DRESSING:
2 teaspoons French mustard
1 teaspoon Worcestershire sauce
2 tablespoons freshly squeezed lemon juice
1 egg, beaten
salt and pepper to taste

Serves 4
Preparation time: 15 minutes
Cooking time: 10 minutes
Freezing: Not recommended

1. Rub the inside of 4 small salad bowls with one of the cloves of garlic.
2. Chop the others and slowly heat in 3 tablespoons of the oil for about 5 minutes; do not allow it to burn. Discard.
3. Toss the bread in the oil, spread on a baking sheet and bake in a preheated oven, 190°C/375°F, for 10 minutes, until crisp. Leave to cool.
4. Whisk the dressing ingredients together with the remaining oil.
5. Place the lettuce in the bowls, sprinkle over the cheese and pour in the dressing. Toss well, sprinkle with the croûtons and serve immediately.

PASTA WITH TOMATO SAUCE AND ZUCCHINI

250 g (8 oz) fresh fettuccine or 175 g (6 oz) dried spaghetti
2 tablespoons butter
2 cloves garlic, crushed
2 tablespoons olive oil
350 g (12 oz) zucchini, cut into thin sticks
50 g (2 oz) Parmesan cheese, grated (optional)

FOR THE SAUCE:
1 tablespoon olive oil
1 onion, chopped
500 g (1 lb) tomatoes, skinned, seeded and sliced
300 ml (1¼ cups) tomato juice
2 tablespoons dry vermouth
salt and pepper to taste

1. First prepare the sauce. Heat the oil in a pan, add the onion and sauté for 5 minutes. Add the remaining ingredients, cover and simmer for 15 minutes. Keep warm.

2. Cook the pasta according to packet instructions. Drain, rinse and toss in half of the butter and 1 clove garlic. Keep warm.

3. Just before serving, heat the remaining butter and the olive oil in a pan, add the remaining garlic and the zucchini and stir-fry for about 3 minutes, until just tender.

4. Serve the pasta with the sauce, topped with the zucchini. Sprinkle with Parmesan, if you wish.

Serves 4
Preparation time:
15 minutes
Cooking time:
20–25 minutes
Freezing:
Recommended for
sauce only

LEEK, TOMATO AND CHEESE SALAD

6 leeks, sliced
300 ml (1¼ cups) light stock
6 large tomatoes, skinned,
seeded and sliced
250 g (8 oz) Mozzarella
cheese, sliced
FOR THE DRESSING:
4 tablespoons olive or
sunflower oil
2 tablespoons freshly
squeezed orange juice

2 tablespoons wine
vinegar
1 teaspoon coarse-grain
mustard
1 teaspoon liquid honey
3 tablespoons chopped
parsley
1 tablespoon chopped basil
salt and pepper to taste

Serves 6
Preparation time:
15 minutes, plus
chilling
Cooking time:
2 minutes
Freezing:
Not recommended

1. Blanch the leeks in the boiling stock for 2 minutes. Drain, place in a bowl and season with salt and pepper.
2. Mix the dressing ingredients together and toss into the leeks while still warm. Leave to cool, then add the tomatoes. Mix together lightly, then chill until required.
3. Transfer to individual plates, arrange the cheese on top and season lightly with salt and pepper.

WARM SPINACH SALAD

If quails' eggs are unobtainable, use 3 chopped hens' eggs.

500 g (1 lb) young spinach
leaves
1 large head chicory
1 clove garlic, halved
175 g (6 oz) button
mushrooms, sliced
12 quails' eggs,
hard-boiled and halved
FOR THE DRESSING:
2 tablespoons olive oil

1 teaspoons sesame oil
(optional)
175 g (6 oz) bacon,
diced
2 tablespoons fruit wine
vinegar
1 teaspoon coarse-grain
mustard
salt and pepper to taste

Serves 4
Preparation time:
25 minutes
Cooking time:
8 minutes
Freezing:
Not recommended

1. Tear or shred the spinach and chicory leaves.
2. Rub the inside of 4 individual salad bowls or plates with the garlic; discard. Arrange the spinach and chicory in the bowls or plates. Add the mushrooms and eggs.
3. Heat the oil(s) in a pan, add the bacon and fry until crisp. Remove with a slotted spoon; sprinkle on the salad.
4. Add the vinegar, mustard, and salt and pepper to the pan and allow to bubble. Serve hot, separately, for diners to toss on their salad themselves.

HADDOCK AND WHITING TURBAN

This can be prepared in advance—completely ready, just to pop in the oven. Do not cook in advance or the spinach will lose its bright green colour as it stands.

6–8 large spinach or lettuce leaves
500 g (1 lb) whiting fillets, skinned and halved lengthways
750 g (1½ lb) smoked haddock fillets, skinned
2 egg whites
1 teaspoon mild curry powder or paste
1 teaspoon turmeric

1 teaspoon salt
¾ cup whipping cream
pepper to taste
FOR THE SAUCE:
⅔ cup sour cream
2 egg yolks
½ teaspoon Dijon mustard
juice of ½ lemon

Serves 4
Preparation time:
25 minutes, plus chilling
Cooking time:
30 minutes
Freezing:
Not recommended

1. Blanch the spinach or lettuce in boiling water for 30 seconds, or until just limp; drain well.
2. Arrange about 6 whiting fillets, skinned side inwards, alternately with the spinach or lettuce, around the edge of a greased 20 cm (8 inch) ring mould, leaving a few gaps.
3. Place the haddock, remaining whiting, egg whites, curry, turmeric, salt and pepper in a blender or food processor and work until smooth.
4. Chill for 1 hour, then process again, gradually adding the cream.
5. Press the mixture carefully but firmly into the prepared mould. Fold over any spinach or whiting ends. Cover with greased foil.
6. Place in a roasting tin half-filled with water and cook in a preheated oven, 180°C/350°F, for 30 minutes. Drain off the juices and reserve for the sauce. Turn out the Turban onto a serving plate.
7. To make the sauce, place all the ingredients, with the reserved juices and salt and pepper to taste, in a blender or food processor and work until smooth. Heat gently.
8. Serve the Turban hot or cold, with new potatoes and snow peas. Serve the sauce separately.

GUINEA FOWL WITH CUCUMBER

2 tablespoons oil
1 guinea fowl, jointed into
   4 portions
150 ml (²/₃ cup) rosé wine
1 thyme sprig
300 ml (1¼ cups) light stock
6 green onions, sliced

¹/₃ cucumber, peeled, sliced
   and seeded
3 tablespoons cream
1 teaspoon grenadine
   (optional)
salt and pepper to taste

1. Heat the oil in a pan, add the guinea fowl portions and fry until browned. Drain off the oil, then pour in the wine. Add the thyme, and salt and pepper, cover and cook for 15 minutes, turning once. Transfer the guinea fowl to a warmed serving dish and keep warm.

2. Add the stock, onions and cucumber to the pan and cook, uncovered, for 5 minutes. Remove the vegetables with a slotted spoon and arrange on the serving dish.

3. Boil the liquid left in the pan until reduced to about 300 ml (1¼ cups). Stir in the cream and grenadine, if using. Pour over the guinea fowl. Serve with Peas with Lettuce (page 76) and new potatoes.

Serves 4
Preparation time:
15 minutes
Cooking time:
About 35 minutes
Freezing:
Not recommended

ELLA'S ROAST PORK

This is a popular dish of a Portuguese friend of mine. It looks best made with a long rolled joint of pork.

1.5 kg (3 lb) rolled loin or leg of pork, or smoked loin of pork
500 g (1 lb) carrots, sliced thinly
1/3 cup raisins
300 ml (1 1/4 cups) light stock
150 ml (2/3 cup) port
2 tablespoons flour, blended with 1 tablespoon water (optional)

FOR THE MARINADE:
3 tablespoons sunflower oil
1 1/2 tablespoons soy sauce
juice of 1 lemon
1 tablespoon wine vinegar
1 clove garlic, crushed
salt and pepper to taste
TO GARNISH:
50 g (2 oz) pine nuts, toasted

Serves 6
Preparation time:
25 minutes, plus marinating
Cooking time:
About 1 1/2 hours
Freezing:
Recommended

1. Mix the marinade ingredients together and place in a large, strong polythene bag. Add the pork, carrots and raisins and leave overnight.
2. Lift out the pork, then remove the carrots and raisins with a slotted spoon and arrange closely in a line, in a roasting tin. Put the pork on top. Pour in the stock and marinade.
3. Roast in a preheated oven, 170°C/325°F, for about 1 1/2 hours or until tender, basting frequently and topping up with boiling water as necessary.
4. Spoon the carrots and raisins onto a warmed serving platter. Slice the pork and arrange on top.
5. Pour the port into the pan juices and allow to bubble for 2 minutes; if you wish, thicken with the blended flour. Check the seasoning. Pour a little of the sauce over the meat and strain the rest into a jug.
6. Garnish with the pine nuts and serve with Brown Rice with Broccoli, Celery and Nuts (page 78) and spinach.

LAMB WITH WATERCRESS IN FILO

1/3 cup butter
1 small onion, chopped
1 clove garlic, crushed
1 bunch watercress, chopped
2 tablespoons wine
1 kg (2 lb) boned leg of lamb

1 tablespoon oil
1 teaspoon chopped rosemary leaves
50 g (2 oz) Feta cheese, sliced thinly (optional)
4 sheets filo pastry
salt and pepper to taste
rosemary sprigs to garnish

1. Melt a third of the butter in a pan, add the onion and garlic and sauté for 3 minutes. Add the watercress and wine, cover and simmer for 3 minutes. Purée in a blender or food processor and leave to cool.

2. Trim the lamb of all fat and sinews, then cut into 4 long fillets.

3. Heat the oil in a pan, add the lamb, rosemary, and salt and pepper, and fry for 3 minutes on each side. Drain on kitchen paper and leave to cool.

4. Slash the fillets in 4 places, almost through. Fill each slash with cheese, if using, and watercress purée. Spread the remaining purée on top. Season with salt and pepper.

5. Melt the remaining butter and use half to brush the filo sheets. Fold in half, place a fillet on each and wrap up like an envelope. Glaze with the remaining butter.

6. Place on a baking sheet and bake in a preheated oven, 190°C/375°F, for 25 minutes. Serve hot with a green salad and cherry tomatoes. Garnish with rosemary.

Serves 4
Preparation time:
15 minutes, plus cooling time
Cooking time:
25 minutes
Freezing:
Not recommended

PORK DIJONNAISE

2 tablespoons sunflower
  oil
4 large pork loin chops
250 g (8 oz) baby onions
2 cloves garlic, crushed
125 g (4 oz) bacon,
  sliced
300 ml (1¼ cups) dry
  cider

125 g (4 oz) button
  mushrooms, sliced
3 thyme or tarragon sprigs
3 tablespoons coarse-grain
  mustard
⅔ cup sour cream
salt and pepper to taste
thyme sprigs to garnish

Serves 4
Preparation time:
15 minutes
Cooking time:
About 25 minutes
Freezing:
Recommended

1. Heat the oil in a pan, add the chops and cook for 2 minutes on each side. Remove and set aside.
2. Add the onions, garlic and bacon to the pan and sauté for about 3 minutes.
3. Add the cider and boil for 3 minutes, or until reduced by a third. Add the mushrooms, herbs, mustard, and salt and pepper, stir, then cook for 2 minutes.
4. Return the chops to the pan, spoon over the sauce, cover and simmer for about 12 minutes, until tender.
5. Transfer the chops to a warmed serving platter. Stir the cream into the sauce in the pan and reheat gently; do not allow to boil.
6. Spoon the sauce over the chops and garnish with thyme. Serve with noodles, Carrots Sweet and Sour (page 77) and a green vegetable.

APRICOT AMARETTI FOOL

350 g (12 oz) dried
  apricots, soaked
4 tablespoons liquid
  honey
1½ cups yogurt

175 g (6 oz) ratafia
  biscuits, crushed roughly
3 tablespoons brandy
3 egg whites

Serves 4
Preparation time:
10 minutes, plus
soaking time and
chilling
Cooking time:
5 minutes
Freezing:
Not recommended

1. Place the apricots, honey and 2–3 tablespoons of water in a pan and cook for 5 minutes. Leave to cool, then purée in a blender or food processor.
2. Stir in three quarters of the yogurt and biscuits, and the brandy.
3. Whisk the egg whites until stiff, then fold in. Chill until required.
4. Top with the remaining yogurt and sprinkle with the remaining biscuit crumbs to serve.

CHOUX BUNS WITH MANGO CREAM

These choux buns are made with half the usual amount of fat, which makes them light and crisp. Fill just before serving to keep them crisp.

3 tablespoons butter
200 ml (1 cup) water
1 cup flour, sifted
3 eggs, beaten
few slivered almonds

FOR THE FILLING:
2 ripe mangos, peeled
few drops orange flower water (optional)

1 large ripe banana, mashed
1 cup whipping cream, whipped

TO SERVE:
icing sugar to dust
1 kiwi fruit, peeled and sliced

Serves 6
Preparation time:
25 minutes
Cooking time:
About 30 minutes
Freezing:
Recommended for buns only

1. Place the butter and water in a pan and heat gently until melted, then bring to the boil. Add the flour all at once and beat well until the dough leaves the side of the pan. Leave to cool for 10 minutes.
2. Gradually beat in all but 2 tablespoons of the egg, to form a stiff dropping consistency.
3. Drop into 6 mounds on a greased baking sheet, spacing them well apart. Glaze with the remaining egg and sprinkle with the almonds. Bake in a preheated oven, 200°C/400°F, for about 30 minutes, until crisp and golden.
4. Split in half, scrape out any uncooked dough and return to the oven for 2 minutes to crisp. Cool on a wire rack while preparing the filling.
5. Slice one mango and set aside. Purée the other mango, with the orange flower water if using, in a blender or food processor.
6. Mix the banana and cream together and spoon into the bun bases. Trickle over the mango purée, cover with the bun tops and dust with icing sugar.
7. Serve with the sliced mango and kiwi fruit.

APPLES WITH SAUTERNES SAUCE

4 apples, cored
2 tablespoons dark marmalade
1/3 cup raisins

75 g (3 oz) light brown soft sugar
150 ml (2/3 cup) Sauternes wine
1 orange

1. Score the apples round the middle. Place in a shallow ovenproof dish. Mix the marmalade and fruit together and use to fill each cavity.
2. Sprinkle the sugar around, then pour in the wine. Cook in a preheated oven, 190°C/375°F, for 1 hour, basting occasionally.
3. Meanwhile, pare the rind from the orange and cut into shreds. Squeeze the juice and heat gently in a pan.
4. Transfer the apples to a serving dish. Drain off the juices from the cooking dish and stir into the hot orange juice.
5. Decorate the apples with the orange strips and serve with the orange sauce, and cream or yogurt if you wish.

Serves 4
Preparation time:
10 minutes
Cooking time:
1 hour
Freezing:
Recommended

COFFEE AND WALNUT ROULADE

4 eggs, separated
1/2 cup fine sugar
1 tablespoon instant coffee
  powder
1/2 cup walnuts, ground
  finely
fine sugar for sprinkling
walnut halves to decorate

FOR THE FILLING:
1 tablespoon instant coffee
  powder
1 tablespoon hot water
2/3 cup whipping cream,
  whipped
2 tablespoons fine sugar
1 egg white
1 tablespoon whisky

Serves 4
Preparation time:
20 minutes
Cooking time:
20 minutes
Freezing:
Recommended

1. Line a 23 × 30 cm (9 × 12 inch) jelly roll tin with foil and grease lightly.
2. Whisk the egg yolks, sugar and coffee powder together in a bowl over a pan of gently simmering water until thick and creamy. Leave to cool, whisking occasionally.
3. Whisk the egg whites until stiff, then fold gently into the coffee mixture with the ground walnuts.
4. Spoon into the prepared tin and bake in a preheated oven, 180°C/350°F, for 20 minutes.
5. Turn out onto a sheet of waxed paper sprinkled with fine sugar. Carefully peel off the foil and roll up in the paper. Leave to cool while making the filling.
6. Dissolve the coffee in the water. Leave to cool, then whisk into the cream with the sugar.
7. Whisk the egg white until stiff, then fold into the coffee cream with the whisky.
8. Carefully unroll the roulade, remove the paper and spread with most of the filling. Re-roll and decorate with the remaining cream and the walnut halves.

BRANDIED BREAD PUDDING

A sophisticated version of a traditional pudding. A light sauce separates out from the pudding when it is cooked, so cream to serve is unnecessary.

2/3 cup raisins
grated rind and juice of
  1 orange
4 tablespoons brandy
9 slices whole grain bread,
  crusts removed, buttered
  and halved diagonally

600 ml (2 1/2 cups) milk
1/3 cup light brown soft
  sugar
2 eggs, plus 1 yolk
grated nutmeg for
  sprinkling

1. Place the raisins and orange juice in a pan and heat gently for about 2 minutes. Add half of the brandy. Cool for 1 hour.

2. Arrange alternate layers of bread and raisins in a 1.2 litre (5 cup) ovenproof dish. Sprinkle with the remaining brandy.

3. Place the milk, sugar and orange rind in a pan and heat gently.

4. Beat the eggs and yolk in a large bowl, then whisk in the hot milk. Gradually pour over the bread, allowing it to soak in. Set aside for 1 hour or overnight.

5. Sprinkle with nutmeg, place in a roasting tin half-filled with boiling water and cook in a preheated oven, 190°C/ 375°F, for 1 hour, until the pudding is risen and crunchy on top. Serve hot.

Serves 4
Preparation time:
15 minutes, plus cooling and standing time
Cooking time:
1 hour
Freezing:
Not recommended

VEGETARIAN MENUS

MENU FOR FOUR
Artichokes with Avocado Cream, Spinach and Lentil Galette, Brown Bread Ice Cream.
Suggested wines. *Starter:* Verduzzo Del Piave. *Main course:* Corbières or Crozes-Hermitage.

MENU FOR FOUR
Mushroom Croustades, Egg plant Parmigiana, Bananas with Orange and Rum.
Suggested wines. *Starter:* Amontillado sherry. *Main course:* Chianti Classico.

MENU FOR FOUR
Bean and Cashew Nut Salad, Malfatti with Red Pepper Sauce, Soft Fruit Compote with Liqueur Cream.
Suggested wine. Gambellara Superiore 'Il Giangio' throughout the meal.

MENU FOR FOUR
Four Fruit Vinaigrette Salad, Zucchini and Rice Streudels, Raspberry and Nut Meringue.
Suggested wine. *Main course:* Orvieto Secco, or Valpolicella Classico.

ARTICHOKES WITH AVOCADO CREAM

To eat an artichoke, work from the outside in, pulling off the leaves and dipping the fleshy base into the sauce. Eat the fleshy part, then discard the leaves. Eat the heart with a knife and fork. Do not prepare the avocado cream more than 30 minutes in advance.

4 globe artichokes
juice of 1 lemon
1 large avocado, peeled, halved and stoned
3 tablespoons sour cream or natural yogurt
3 tablespoons mayonnaise
2 green onions, chopped
1 teaspoon Worcestershire sauce
salt and pepper to taste
chopped parsley to serve

Serves 4
Preparation time: 20 minutes, plus chilling
Cooking time: 40–50 minutes
Freezing: Not recommended

1. Remove the stalk from the artichokes and trim the leaf tops if you wish. Boil in plenty of salted water, with half of the lemon juice added, for 40–50 minutes, until the base leaves pull off easily. Drain upside down, cool and chill.
2. Part the leaves and remove the centre hairy choke with a teaspoon.
3. Blend the remaining ingredients together to make a smooth cream. Spoon into the centre of each artichoke and sprinkle with parsley to serve.

MUSHROOM CROUSTADES

1 small uncut loaf	*1 tablespoon flour*
¼ cup butter	*200 ml (1 cup) milk*
2 tablespoons oil	*2 tablespoons chopped*
3 tablespoons vegetable	* parsley*
* stock or water*	*1 thyme sprig, chopped*
350 g (12 oz) button	*salt and pepper to taste*
* mushrooms, sliced*	*thyme sprigs to garnish*

Serves 4
Preparation time:
20 minutes
Cooking time:
About 30 minutes
Freezing:
Recommended for
cases only

1. Cut off a thin slice from each end of the loaf and discard. Trim off the crusts and cut the bread into 4 rectangles, 3 cm (1¼ inch) thick, measuring 9 × 5 cm (3½ × 2 inches). Hollow out the centre of each piece, leaving a shell about 1 cm (½ inch) thick.
2. Melt three quarters of the butter with the oil and lightly brush the top of the cases. Place on a baking sheet, buttered side up, and bake in a preheated oven, 170°C/325°F, for about 30 minutes, until crisp and golden. Drain on kitchen paper.
3. Meanwhile, melt the remaining butter in a pan, add the stock or water, mushrooms and flour, cover, shake well and simmer for 5 minutes. Stir in the milk, herbs, and salt and pepper and simmer for 1 minute.
4. Divide between the croustades and serve immediately, garnished with thyme.

FOUR-FRUIT VINAIGRETTE SALAD

1 ripe paw-paw, peeled,	*½ honeydew melon,*
* seeded and cut into*	* peeled, seeded and cut*
* chunks*	* into chunks*
1 large pear, peeled, cored	*4–6 tablespoons*
* and cut into chunks*	* vinaigrette dressing*
2 large grapefruit, peeled	*1 tablespoon chopped mint*
* and cut into segments*	*mint sprigs to garnish*

Serves 4
Preparation time:
20 minutes, plus
chilling
Freezing:
Not recommended

1. Mix the fruits together in a bowl. Pour over the dressing, sprinkle with the mint and toss well.
2. Transfer to sundae or small glass dishes and chill until required. Garnish with mint to serve.

VARIATION
Slice the fruits and arrange on individual serving plates. Mix the dressing and mint together and trickle over the fruits. Chill and garnish with mint to serve.

BEAN AND CASHEW NUT SALAD

125 g (4 oz) dried white beans, soaked overnight
½ small bulb fennel or 2 celery sticks, sliced thinly
1 red apple, cored and cut into chunks
3 green onions, sliced
50 g (2 oz) roasted salted cashew nuts

FOR THE DRESSING:
4 tablespoons sunflower oil
juice of 1 lemon
1 tablespoon wine vinegar
1 tablespoon sweet sherry
½ teaspoon dried thyme
1 teaspoon coarse-grain mustard
salt and pepper to taste
TO SERVE:
4 large radicchio or lettuce leaves

Serves 4
Preparation time: 15 minutes, plus soaking time
Cooking time: About 1 hour
Freezing: Recommended for beans only

1. Drain the beans, place in a pan and cover with cold water. Bring to the boil and boil rapidly for 10 minutes, then lower the heat and simmer for about 50 minutes or until tender; drain.
2. Place the dressing ingredients in a screw-top jar, shake well to blend, then pour over the warm beans in a bowl.
3. When cold, mix with the remaining salad ingredients.
4. Arrange the radicchio or lettuce leaves on individual serving plates and top with the salad to serve.

MALFATTI WITH RED PEPPER SAUCE

Malfatti are light Italian spinach dumplings.

500 g (1 lb) spinach
1 onion, chopped finely
1 clove garlic, crushed
1 tablespoon olive oil
350 g (12 oz) Ricotta or cottage cheese
3 eggs, beaten
⅔ cup dried breadcrumbs
½ cup whole wheat flour
1 teaspoon salt
50 g (2 oz) Parmesan cheese, grated

grated nutmeg to taste
2 tablespoons butter, melted
FOR THE SAUCE:
2 red peppers
2 tablespoons oil
1 onion, chopped
397 g (14 oz) can chopped tomatoes
150 ml (⅔ cup) water
salt and pepper to taste

1. First prepare the sauce. Place the peppers under a broiler until the skins blacken and blister. Leave to cool, then remove the skin and seeds. Chop the flesh.

2. Heat the oil in a pan, add the onion and peppers and sauté for 5 minutes. Add the tomatoes, water, and salt and pepper, cover and simmer for 15 minutes. Purée in a blender or food processor, then rub through a sieve. Keep warm.

3. Remove any large stalks from the spinach, then blanch the leaves in boiling water for 1 minute. Drain well, squeeze dry, then chop finely.

4. Mix with the onion, garlic, oil, Ricotta or cottage cheese, eggs, breadcrumbs, flour, salt, half of the Parmesan, and pepper and nutmeg. Roll into 24 small 'logs' with wet hands, or shape into 12–16 ovals (quenelles) using 2 dessertspoons.

5. Drop in batches into gently boiling salted water and cook for 5 minutes. Remove, drain and toss in the butter.

6. Arrange on individual plates, on a pool of the sauce. Sprinkle with the remaining Parmesan to serve.

Serves 4
Preparation time:
30 minutes
Cooking time:
30 minutes
Freezing:
Not recommended

SPINACH AND LENTIL GALETTE

FOR THE PANCAKES:
1/2 cup whole wheat or
  buckwheat flour
1/2 cup all-purpose flour
pinch of salt
2 eggs
300 ml (1 1/4 cups) milk
FOR THE 1ST FILLING:
1 bulb fennel, sliced thinly
1 onion, chopped
175 g (6 oz) red lentils
3 tomatoes, skinned and
  chopped
450 ml (1 3/4 cups) vegetable
  stock

1 tablespoon chopped
  marjoram
FOR THE 2ND FILLING:
2 tablespoons butter
500 g (1 lb) spinach,
  shredded
1 onion, chopped
1 clove garlic, crushed
250 g (8 oz) Ricotta or
  cottage cheese
salt, pepper and grated
  nutmeg to taste
TO FINISH:
50 g (2 oz) Parmesan
  cheese, grated

Serves 4
Preparation time:
35 minutes
Cooking time:
1 hour
Freezing:
Recommended

1. Place the ingredients for the first filling in a pan and simmer for 25 minutes, until pulpy. Add salt and pepper.
2. Meanwhile, make the pancakes. Place the dry ingredients in a bowl and make a well in the centre. Add the eggs and half of the milk, then gradually mix in the flour to make a smooth batter. Stir in the remaining milk and beat for 2–3 minutes. Alternatively, place half of the flour and the remaining ingredients in a blender or food processor and work for 30 seconds. Add the remaining flour and blend for 30 seconds.
3. Lightly oil an 18 cm (7 inch) heavy-based frying pan and place over a high heat. When hot, pour in enough batter to cover the base. Cook until the edge is golden and bubbles appear on the surface, then turn and cook the other side until golden. Turn onto a plate and cover while cooking the remaining batter, to make 14 pancakes.
4. To make the second filling, melt the butter in a pan, add the spinach, onion and garlic and cook for about 5 minutes, until wilted and just tender. Season with salt, pepper and nutmeg and stir in the cheese.
5. Lightly grease a 20 cm (8 inch) round deep cake tin and line the base and side with pancakes, cutting to fit.
6. Cover the base with a layer of the first filling, top with a pancake, sprinkle lightly with Parmesan, then cover with a layer of the second filling. Repeat the layers, finishing with a pancake.
7. Cover with greased foil and steam or boil for 1 hour.
8. Cut into wedges and serve with tomato sauce (see page 22) and broccoli.

ZUCCHINI AND RICE STREUDELS

Although it looks very fragile, filo pastry is in fact quite easy
to use.

1/4 cup butter
250 g (8 oz) zucchini,
grated
1 onion, chopped
1 clove garlic, crushed
1 cup brown rice,
cooked
1/2 cup slivered almonds,
toasted
1 egg, beaten

4 tablespoons table cream
50 g (2 oz) Parmesan
cheese, grated
1/2 teaspoon dried thyme
8 sheets frozen filo pastry,
thawed
sesame seeds for sprinkling
salt and pepper to taste

Serves 4
Preparation time:
45 minutes, plus
chilling
Cooking time:
25 minutes
Freezing:
Recommended

1. Melt half of the butter in a pan, add the zucchini, onion
and garlic, cover and cook for 5 minutes.
2. Transfer to a bowl, add the rice, almonds, egg, cream,
Parmesan, thyme, and salt and pepper and mix well. Leave
to cool, then chill for 30 minutes.
3. Melt the remaining butter. Allowing 2 sheets of filo
pastry per streudel, brush one filo sheet with butter, then
top with the other. Spread a quarter of the filling lengthways along one side of the filo, then roll up.
4. Brush the edges of the filo with butter to seal, then
brush the streudel all over to glaze and roll loosely into a
coil. Sprinkle with sesame seeds. Repeat with the remaining filo and filling.
5. Bake in a preheated oven, 190°C/375°F, for 25 minutes.
Serve hot with salad.

EGG PLANT PARMIGIANA

1 kg (2 lb) egg plants,
sliced
150 ml (2/3 cup) olive oil
(approximately)
2 large onions, chopped
250 g (8 oz) carrots,
chopped
3 celery sticks, chopped
1 green pepper, cored,
seeded and chopped
2 cloves garlic, crushed

2 teaspoons coriander
seeds, crushed
1 teaspoon dried thyme
150 ml (2/3 cup) red or
white wine
2 × 397 g (14 oz) cans
chopped tomatoes
500 g (1 lb) Mozzarella
cheese, chopped
125 g (4 oz) Parmesan
cheese, grated
salt and pepper to taste

1. Arrange the egg plant slices in layers in a colander, sprinkling each layer with salt. Leave to stand for about 30 minutes, then rinse and pat dry with kitchen paper.

2. Heat 5 tablespoons oil in a large frying pan and fry the egg plants in batches: brush the slices with oil as necessary, and add a little water to each batch; cook until softened. Drain on kitchen paper.

3. Heat another 2 tablespoons oil in the pan, add the vegetables and garlic and fry for 10 minutes. Add the coriander, thyme and wine and cook for 5 minutes. Add the tomatoes, season well with salt and pepper, cover and simmer for 20 minutes.

4. Arrange the egg plant slices, tomato sauce and cheeses in alternate layers in a 2.75 litre (12 cup) casserole dish, finishing with cheese; reserve a little of both cheeses.

5. Cover and cook in a preheated oven, 190°C/375°F, for about 1 hour; uncover for the last 20 minutes and top with the reserved cheese.

6. Serve with crusty garlic bread and a green salad or green vegetables.

Serves 4
Preparation time:
40 minutes, plus standing time
Cooking time:
About 1 hour
Freezing:
Recommended

SOFT FRUIT COMPOTE WITH LIQUEUR CREAM

Don't blanch at the thought of eating flowers – these are quite harmless and look lovely.

500 g (1 lb) mixed soft fruits, e.g. peaches, apricots, strawberries, kiwi fruit
3 tablespoons fine sugar
3 tablespoons liqueur, e.g. Galliano, kirsch, Grand Marnier, Drambuie

grated rind and juice of 1 orange
1 egg white
2/3 cup whipping cream, whipped
borage or violet flowers (optional)

Serves 4
Preparation time: 15 minutes, plus macerating
Freezing: Not recommended

1. Place the prepared fruits in a glass bowl; cut into spoon-sized pieces if necessary. Sprinkle with the sugar, 1 tablespoon of the liqueur and the orange juice. Cover and leave to macerate for about 2 hours.
2. Whisk the egg white until stiff, then fold into the cream with the remaining liqueur and the orange rind.
3. Decorate the fruit with flowers, if you wish, and serve with the liqueur cream.

BROWN BREAD ICE CREAM

This is one of our oldest ice creams, originating in the
eighteenth century.

*1 cup fresh whole wheat
   breadcrumbs, toasted
6 egg yolks
1 cup light brown soft
   sugar*

*300 ml (1¼ cups) milk
1 cup table cream
1 teaspoon vanilla extract*

1. Crush the toasted breadcrumbs with a rolling pin until
fine.
2. Whisk the egg yolks and sugar together. Place the milk,
cream and vanilla extract in a pan and heat until almost
boiling, then·pour from a height onto the egg yolks,
whisking constantly.
3. Return to a very low heat, stirring constantly, until the
thickness of table cream; do not allow to boil. Leave to
cool, then chill thoroughly.
4. Stir in the breadcrumbs, turn into a shallow freezerproof container, cover, seal and freeze for about 6–8
hours, until firm; stir occasionally during freezing.
5. Transfer to the refrigerator 20 minutes before serving
to soften. Scoop into glass dishes and serve with a fruit
compote, e.g. blackberry and apple, if you wish.

Serves 4
Preparation time:
10 minutes
Cooking time:
10 minutes
Freezing time:
6–8 hours

BANANAS WITH ORANGE AND RUM

*4 large ripe bananas,
    sliced thickly
grated rind and juice of
    1 large orange
2 tablespoons butter*

*3 tablespoons light brown
    soft sugar
2 tablespoons rum
ground cinnamon to
    sprinkle
chopped walnuts to serve*

Serves 4
Preparation time:
10 minutes
Cooking time:
15–20 minutes
Freezing:
Not recommended

1. Place the bananas in 4 ovenproof ramekins.
2. Place the orange rind and juice, butter and sugar in a pan and heat gently until melted, then stir in the rum.
3. Pour over the bananas, sprinkle with cinnamon and bake in a preheated oven, 180°C/350°F, for 15–20 minutes, until just soft. Sprinkle with walnuts and serve warm.

RASPBERRY AND NUT MERINGUE

Prepare the meringue rounds and filling in advance, but assemble the gâteau 1 hour before serving, to keep the meringue crisp.

*3 egg whites
1 cup light brown soft
    sugar
75 g (3 oz) hazelnuts or
    walnuts, ground finely
500 g (1 lb) raspberries*

*113 g (4 oz) cream
    cheese
227 g (8 oz) carton
    skimmed milk soft cheese
2 tablespoons icing sugar*

Serves 4
Preparation time:
20 minutes
Cooking time:
40–50 minutes
Freezing:
Recommended for
meringue rounds
only

1. Cut 3 pieces of foil to fit baking sheets or upturned roasting tins and grease lightly.
2. Whisk the egg whites until stiff, then whisk in the sugar until smooth, glossy and very stiff. Fold in the ground nuts.
3. Spread into three 20 cm (8 inch) circles on the foil.
4. Bake in a preheated oven, 170°C/325°F, for 40–50 minutes, until crisp on top; this may have to be done in batches.
5. Turn the meringues upside down on a wire rack and carefully peel off the foil in strips while warm.
6. Reserve a quarter of the raspberries. Place the rest in a blender or food processor with the soft cheeses and icing sugar and work until smooth.
7. Sandwich the 3 meringues together with two thirds of the raspberry mixture. Spread the rest on the top and decorate with the reserved raspberries.

ITALIAN-STYLE DINNER FOR FOUR

This is a good 'prepare ahead' dinner—the main course simply needs rice or pasta to serve. If fresh peaches are unavailable for the sorbet, use canned ones in natural juice; use the juice instead of water in the recipe.

MENU

Peperonata with Prosciutto, Chicken with Fennel Ragù, Peach Sorbet with Fruit Coulis.

Suggested wines. *Starter:* Villa Antinori Bianco, or Montilla Dry. *Main course:* Verdicchio Classico.

PEPERONATA WITH PROSCIUTTO

Peppers assume a delicious smoky flavour when broiled or roasted, which nicely complements the salty tang of prosciutto ham.

2 large red peppers
2 large green peppers
½ cup raisins
6 thin slices prosciutto ham, halved lengthways
FOR THE DRESSING:
3 tablespoons olive oil

1½ tablespoons wine or cider vinegar
1 clove garlic, crushed
1 teaspoon Dijon mustard
¼ teaspoon salt
black pepper to taste

Serves 4
Preparation time: 10 minutes, plus chilling
Cooking time: 30 minutes
Freezing: Not recommended

1. Place the peppers on a baking sheet and roast in a preheated oven, 220°C/425°F, for about 30 minutes, turning occasionally, until the skins start to blacken and blister. Leave to cool, then peel, core and slice. Place in a bowl with the raisins.
2. Whisk the dressing ingredients together, pour over the peppers and raisins and mix well. Cover and chill until required.
3. Roll up the ham slices and arrange on individual plates with the pepper and raisin salad.

CHICKEN WITH FENNEL RAGÙ

4 chicken quarters
whole wheat flour to coat
2 tablespoons olive oil
2 tablespoons butter
2 bulbs fennel, sliced
4 leeks, sliced thinly
1 clove garlic, crushed
300 ml (1¼ cups) dry
   white wine or cider
125 g (4 oz) baby button
   mushrooms

500 g (1 lb) tomato
   sauce
1 tablespoon chopped
   marjoram
4 tablespoons chopped
   parsley
salt and pepper to taste
½ cup slivered almonds,
   toasted
fennel sprigs to garnish

Serves 4
Preparation time:
15 minutes
Cooking time:
About 50 minutes
Freezing:
Recommended

1. Coat the chicken in the flour. Heat the oil in a pan, add the chicken and fry until evenly browned. Set aside.
2. Add the butter, fennel, leek, garlic and 2 tablespoons water to the pan, cover and cook for 10–15 minutes.
3. Add the wine or cider and simmer, uncovered, until reduced by half, then add mushrooms, tomato sauce, herbs and salt and pepper. Return the chicken to the pan, cover and simmer gently for about 30 minutes until cooked.
4. Sprinkle with the almonds, garnish with fennel and serve with rice or pasta.

PEACH SORBET WITH FRUIT COULIS

500 g (1 lb) peaches,
*   skinned and stoned*
grated rind and juice of
*   1 lemon*
2 tablespoons brandy
*   (optional)*

¹/₂ cup sugar
300 ml (1¹/₄ cups) water
250 g (8 oz) redcurrants
sugar to taste
strawberries or raspberries
*   to serve (optional)*

1. Place the peaches, lemon rind and juice, and brandy if using, in a blender or food processor and work until smooth.
2. Place the sugar and water in a pan and heat gently until dissolved, then boil for 5 minutes. Stir into the purée and leave to cool. Turn into a freezerproof container, cover, seal and freeze for about 2 hours, until partially frozen. Beat until slushy, then return to the freezer until firm.
3. Meanwhile, stew the redcurrants with a little water and sugar to taste until soft and pulpy. Rub through a nylon sieve and leave to cool.
4. Transfer the sorbet to the refrigerator about 20 minutes before serving, to soften. Scoop into individual glass dishes and serve with the redcurrant sauce, and strawberries or raspberries if wished.

Serves 4
Preparation time:
25 minutes
Freezing time:
About 4 hours

EASTERN MEDITERRANEAN-STYLE DINNER FOR FOUR

The starter with its lovely colours should be a good talking point! Try and use a brightly coloured melon such as Charentais or watermelon. The kebabs could be skewered ready to be broiled just before sitting down. Serve them with a colourful mixed salad, and rice or a garlic-buttered sesame seed loaf.

MENU
Feta and Melon Salad, Souvlakia, Rosewater Cherries.
Suggested wines. Retsina Kourtaki—an acquired taste, so serve Alsace Riesling as well.

FETA AND MELON SALAD

*1 small ripe melon or
 ¼ watermelon
100 g (3½ oz) pack
 Salad Mix with frisé,
 radicchio, etc*

*200 g (7 oz) Feta cheese
12 small black olives
4 tablespoons vinaigrette
 dressing*

Serves 4
Preparation time:
20 minutes, plus chilling
Freezing:
Not recommended

1. De-seed, peel and cut the melon into about 16 thin wedges.
2. Shred the salad mix and arrange on 4 individual plates.
3. Cut the cheese into 16 fingers, each about 3.5 cm (1½ inches) long.
4. Arrange the cheese, melon and olives around the salad. Trickle over the dressing and chill lightly before serving.

SOUVLAKIA

*750 g (1½ lb) boned leg of
 lamb, cut into 2.5 cm
 (1 inch) cubes
1 onion, grated
4 tablespoons chopped
 parsley*

*juice of ½ lemon
1 teaspoon ground cumin
1 teaspoon paprika
1 onion, quartered
salt and pepper to taste*

Serves 4
Preparation time:
10 minutes, plus marinating
Cooking time:
About 15 minutes
Freezing:
Recommended at end of stage 2

1. Place all the ingredients, except the quartered onion, in a bowl, cover and leave to marinate for at least 2 hours. Remove the lamb with a slotted spoon.
2. Separate the onion quarters into segments and thread on 4 long skewers alternately with the meat.
3. Cook the kebabs under a broiler for about 15 minutes, basting occasionally with the marinade, until tender. Serve with rice and a tomato and cucumber salad.

ROSEWATER CHERRIES

500 g (1 lb) fresh, or
  425 g (15 oz) can,
  black cherries, pitted
1½ tablespoons triple
  strength rosewater
½ teaspoon ground
  ginger

½ teaspoon ground
  cinnamon
1 tablespoon liquid honey
240 g (8 oz) carton yogurt
few unsalted pistachios,
  chopped

1. If using fresh cherries, simmer with about 150 ml (⅔ cup) water and sugar to taste for about 5 minutes. If using canned cherries, drain off all but 2 tablespoons of the syrup.
2. Stir in the rosewater, then chill until required.
3. Stir the spices and honey into the yogurt.
4. Divide the cherries between individual serving dishes and top with the yogurt. Sprinkle with the chopped pistachios to serve.

Serves 4
Preparation time:
5–10 minutes, plus chilling
Freezing:
Not recommended

FAR EASTERN-STYLE DINNER FOR FOUR

The saté and sea bass can be prepared ahead to the cooking stage, then finished off before the guests arrive. Sea bass has a superb flavour and texture, but is quite expensive; mullet, bream or haddock could be substituted. Serve with rice, carrot julienne and stir-fried broccoli. If available, use jasmine flowers to decorate the dessert, for an effective finish.

MENU
Pork Saté, Chinese-baked Sea Bass, Lychee and China Tea Sorbet.
Suggested wine. Frascati Secco, or Jasmine tea if you prefer.

PORK SATÉ

350 g (12 oz) pork escalopes or tenderloin
salt and pepper to taste
FOR THE MARINADE:
2 tablespoons fruit chutney
1 tablespoon soy sauce
2 tablespoons oil
1 teaspoon chilli powder
½ teaspoon ground cumin
1 clove garlic, crushed

FOR THE SAUCE:
¼ cup dry roasted peanuts, ground
1 clove garlic, crushed
3 tablespoons wine vinegar
pinch of sugar
1 tablespoon water
TO SERVE:
shredded lettuce

Serves 4
Preparation time: 10 minutes, plus marinating
Cooking time: 6–8 minutes
Freezing: Not recommended

1. Mix the marinade ingredients together in a dish.
2. Cut the escalopes in half lengthways; if using tenderloin, cut in half then slice each half lengthways to give 4 long slices. Add to the marinade, cover and chill for 4 hours.
3. Mix the sauce ingredients together in a bowl, then transfer to a small serving dish.
4. Remove the pork from the marinade with a slotted spoon and pleat onto 4 skewers. Season with salt and pepper and cook under a broiler for 3–4 minutes on each side, until tender.
5. Arrange the shredded lettuce on 4 individual serving plates and place the kebabs on top. Serve immediately, accompanied by the saté sauce.

CHINESE-BAKED SEA BASS

*1 sea bass, weighing about
   1 kg (2 lb), cleaned
2 teaspoons corn starch,
   blended with 200 ml
   (1 cup) fish stock or
   water
2 carrots, cut into julienne
   strips
3 green onions, shredded
FOR THE MARINADE:
2 tablespoons sunflower oil*

*1 teaspoon sesame oil
   (optional)
1 tablespoon shredded
   fresh root ginger
3 green onions, sliced
2 tablespoons light soy
   sauce
pinch of sugar
salt to taste*

Serves 4
Preparation time:
10 minutes, plus
marinating
Cooking time:
About 40 minutes
Freezing:
Not recommended

1. Make 3 slashes on each side of the fish and place on a large sheet of foil. Mix the marinade ingredients together, pour over the fish and rub well in. Fold the foil to form a parcel, sealing well, and leave to marinate for 2 hours.
2. Bake in a preheated oven, 180°C/350°F, for about 40 minutes, until cooked and firm. Transer the fish to a large warmed serving platter and keep warm. Drain the juices into a pan. Add the blended corn starch and bring to the boil, stirring.
3. Add the carrots and onions and simmer for 2 minutes. Pour over the fish and serve immediately, with rice.

LYCHEE AND CHINA TEA SORBET

500 g (1 lb) lychees, peeled and stoned
2 Earl Grey or Jasmine tea bags
1 cup sugar
grated rind and juice of 1 lemon
2 egg whites
jasmine flowers to decorate (optional)

1. Purée the lychees in a blender or food processor. Strain, reserving the juice, and squeezing the pulp dry; you should have 300 ml (1¼ cups) juice.
2. Infuse the tea bags in 600 ml (2½ cups) boiling water for 10 minutes; remove the tea bags.
3. Dissolve the sugar in the tea, add the lemon rind and juice and simmer for 5 minutes. Leave to cool.
4. Mix in the lychee juice, then pour into a shallow freezerproof container, cover, seal and freeze for about 2 hours, until half-frozen and slushy.
5. Whisk the egg whites until soft peaks form. Beat the half-frozen purée to break down the ice crystals, then fold in the egg whites.
6. Cover, seal and freeze for 3 hours, until firm. Transfer to the refrigerator 20 minutes before serving, to soften. Decorate with jasmine flowers, if wished.

Serves 4
Preparation time: 30 minutes
Freezing time: About 5 hours

SCANDINAVIAN-STYLE DINNER FOR SIX

An inexpensive meal that can all be prepared ahead. If you can't get herrings, use small mackerel, although they may be tricky to roll up. Serve the meatballs with a tomato salad, for colour. Kissel can be served with cream.

MENU
Marinated Herrings, Pork Balls with Spinach Sauce, Kissel.
Suggested drinks. *Starter:* schnapps or vodka. *Main course:* strong dry cider or Fitou le Carla.

MARINATED HERRINGS

*250 ml (1 cup) dry white
   wine
3 tablespoons wine or
   cider vinegar
1 onion, sliced thinly
1 carrot, sliced
1 bayleaf*

*bouquet garni of thyme,
   parsley and dill
6 small herrings, heads
   removed and boned
juice of 1 small lemon
salt and pepper to taste
dill sprigs to garnish*

Serves 6
Preparation time:
15 minutes, plus
marinating
Cooking time:
About 15 minutes
Freezing:
Recommended

1. Place the wine, vinegar, onion, carrot, bayleaf and bouquet garni in a pan and bring to the boil. Simmer, uncovered, for 5 minutes.
2. Meanwhile, season the flesh of the fish with salt and pepper and sprinkle with lemon juice. Roll up each herring from the neck to the tail and secure with a wooden cocktail stick.
3. Place the rolled herrings in a shallow ovenproof dish and pour over the wine mixture. Cover with foil and cook in a preheated oven, 220°C/425°F, for about 15 minutes or until cooked. Leave in the marinade to cool overnight.
4. Remove the rolled herrings from the marinade with a slotted spoon and transfer to individual serving plates. Garnish with dill sprigs and serve with thinly sliced whole grain bread.

Illustrated below
right: Pork Balls
with Spinach
Sauce (page 62)

PORK BALLS WITH SPINACH SAUCE

*6 slices whole grain bread,
crusts removed
125 g (4 oz) bacon,
chopped finely
6 tablespoons chopped
parsley
1 kg (2 lb) minced pork
1 egg, beaten
175 g (6 oz) Gruyère or
Emmental cheese, cut
into 24 cubes
3 tablespoons oil
FOR THE SAUCE:
1 large onion, chopped
2 cloves garlic, crushed
1 teaspoon ground cumin*

*2 tablespoons whole wheat
flour
900 ml (3²/3 cups) chicken
stock, or half stock and
half dry cider
500 g (1 lb) spinach, stalks
removed, shredded
²/3 cup sour cream
salt and pepper to taste
TO SERVE:
500 g (1 lb) noodles,
cooked
50 g (2 oz) bacon, broiled
crisply and chopped
parsley sprigs to garnish*

Serves 6
Preparation time:
25 minutes
Cooking time:
20 minutes
Freezing:
Recommended

Illustrated on
page 61

1. Cover the bread with cold water and soak for 5 minutes, then squeeze dry.
2. Mix with the bacon, parsley, pork, egg, and salt and pepper.
3. With wet hands, divide and shape the mixture into 24 patties. Press a cheese cube into the centre and re-form into balls.
4. Heat the oil in a pan, add the pork balls in batches and brown quickly. Transfer to a roasting tin and cook in a preheated oven, 190°C/375°F, for 20 minutes.
5. Meanwhile make the sauce: add the onion and garlic to the pan and sauté for about 5 minutes, to soften. Add the cumin and fry for 1 minute, then add the flour and fry for 1 minute.
6. Gradually stir in the stock, or stock and cider, and bring to the boil, stirring. Season with salt and pepper and add the spinach. Cover and simmer for 5 minutes.
7. Purée in a blender or food processor until smooth, then rub through a sieve to make a really smooth sauce. Reheat gently, whisking in the sour cream.
8. Transfer the pork balls to a plate lined with noodles. Pour over some sauce and sprinkle with the bacon. Garnish with parsley. Hand the remaining sauce separately.

KISSEL

For a traditional Kissel, the fruit is strained through a jelly bag. I prefer to leave the fruit whole, rather than strain it—to keep the texture and fibre.

500 g (1 lb) raspberries
500 g (1 lb) redcurrants or
  blackcurrants
300 ml (1¼ cups) water

½ cup sugar
3 tablespoons potato flour
  or arrowroot, blended
  with a little water

1. Place the fruit, water and sugar in a pan and cook gently for 10–15 minutes, until soft and pulpy.
2. Stir in the blended potato flour or arrowroot and bring back to the boil, stirring until thickened. Leave to cool, then spoon into glass dishes and chill in a refrigerator until required.
3. Serve with pouring cream and cookies if wished.

Serves 6
Preparation time:
5 minutes, plus chilling
Cooking time:
10–15 minutes
Freezing:
Not recommended

SCOTTISH-STYLE DINNER FOR FOUR

The shrimp can be prepared ahead and cooked just before serving. The other two courses can be made beforehand. Serve the pheasant with creamed potatoes and turnips mixed together, and a green vegetable, such as Cabbage with Lemon and Caraway (page 76). Flummery is nice on its own, but is well complemented by a little fresh or stewed fruit.

MENU

Whisky Shrimp, Pheasant Salmis, Honey and Almond Flummery.

Suggested wines. *First course:* Dry sherry if you wish—but a drink is not really required! *Main course:* Côtes du Rhône Villages, Barolo Riserva Speciale Villa Doria.

WHISKY SHRIMP

A quick and easy starter with a delicious flavour. If you can obtain fresh shrimp, so much the better. If not, use frozen peeled shrimp and defrost thoroughly before use.

2 tablespoons butter
2 shallots or 1 small onion, chopped
500 g (1 lb) peeled shrimp
2 tablespoons whisky
2 tablespoons chopped parsley
3 tablespoons sour cream
salt, pepper and ground mace to taste

Serves 4
Preparation time:
5 minutes
Cooking time:
10 minutes
Freezing:
Not recommended

1. Melt the butter in a pan, add the shallots or onion and sauté for about 3 minutes.
2. Add the shrimp and heat gently for 2 minutes. Add the whisky and cook for 1 minute.
3. Add the parsley and sour cream and heat through gently. Season with salt, pepper and mace.
4. Transfer the shrimp with a slotted spoon to 4 individual serving plates. Simmer the sauce until reduced by a third, then spoon over the shrimp. Serve immediately, with thinly sliced whole grain bread.

PHEASANT SALMIS

4 tablespoons olive oil
1 large or 2 small
   pheasants
1 carrot and 1 small
   onion, chopped finely
2 celery sticks, chopped
75 g (3 oz) mushrooms,
   chopped finely

2 tablespoons flour
900 ml (3²/₃ cups) chicken
   stock
300 ml (1¼ cups) red wine
1 teaspoon tomato paste
bouquet garni of bayleaf,
   thyme and parsley
salt and pepper to taste
watercress to garnish

Serves 4
Preparation time:
30 minutes
Cooking time:
45–55 minutes
Freezing:
Recommended

1. Rub 2 tablespoons of the oil over the pheasants and season with salt and pepper. Cook in a preheated oven, 200°C/400°F, for 25 minutes
2. Meanwhile, heat the remaining oil in a pan, add the vegetables and sauté for 5 minutes. Stir in the flour and cook for 2 minutes. Add the remaining ingredients and bring to the boil, stirring. Simmer for 15 minutes.
3. Cut the pheasants in half along the backbone, or into quarters if using 1 large pheasant.
4. Strain the sauce over the pheasants and return to the oven for 20–30 minutes or until cooked. Garnish with watercress to serve.

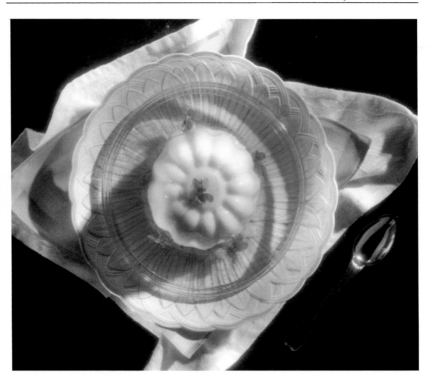

HONEY AND ALMOND FLUMMERY

1.2 litres (5 cups) milk
6 tablespoons liquid honey
125 g (4 oz) ground
  almonds
1 teaspoon almond
  extract
2 teaspoons orange flower
  water

2 envelopes gelatine
6 tablespoons very hot
  water
TO DECORATE:
strips of orange rind or
  violet flowers

1. Place the milk, honey, ground almonds, almond extract and orange flower water in a pan and simmer for 2 minutes. Leave to cool.

2. Sprinkle the gelatine onto the hot water and stir briskly until dissolved. Stir into the almond milk, then pour into 4 lightly oiled 300 ml (1¼ cup) moulds and chill for about 6–8 hours, until set.

3. To turn out, dip the mould briefly into hot water and shake out onto a plate. Decorate with orange rind strips or violets. Serve with fresh raspberries or lightly stewed blackberries and apples, if you wish.

Serves 4
Preparation time:
5 minutes
Setting time:
About 6–8 hours
Freezing:
Not recommended

VALENTINE DINNER FOR TWO

The starter does need a little last-minute attention, but this can always be done together! If you can't find scallops, use large shrimp instead. The other two courses can be prepared ahead. Serve the chicken with buttered parsley rice or pasta bows and a tomato (love apple) salad—with no garlic!

MENU
Scallop and Avocado Gratin, Declarations of Intent, Pink Passion Crush.
Suggested wines. Sparkling Saumur, Anjou, Rosé Champagne or the best Champagne you can afford.

SCALLOP AND AVOCADO GRATIN

150 ml (²/3 cup) fish stock or water
150 ml (²/3 cup) dry white wine
1 small onion, sliced
1 bay leaf
6 peppercorns
6 scallops, sliced
8 baby button mushrooms

1 teaspoon corn starch, blended with
1 tablespoon water
2 tablespoons cream
¹/2 avocado, peeled and sliced
2 teaspoons grated cheese
2 teaspoons dried breadcrumbs
salt to taste

Serves 2
Preparation time:
10 minutes
Cooking time:
15 minutes
Freezing:
Not recommended

1. Place the stock or water, wine, onion, bay leaf, peppercorns and salt in a pan and boil for about 7 minutes, until reduced to 150 ml (²/3 cup).
2. Add the scallops and mushrooms, cover and cook gently for 3–4 minutes until tender. Transfer the scallops and mushrooms to 2 large ovenproof scallop shells with a slotted spoon, cover and keep warm.
3. Add the blended corn starch to the stock, bring to the boil, stirring, then simmer for 1 minute, until thickened. Strain, then stir in the cream.
4. Arrange 2 or 3 avocado slices on each shell, pour over the sauce, cover and keep warm until required.
5. Sprinkle with the cheese and breadcrumbs and place under a broiler to brown. Serve immediately.

DECLARATIONS OF INTENT

*2 boneless chicken breasts,
  each weighing 150 g
  (5 oz), skinned
2 slices Parma ham
2 thin slices Gruyère cheese
1/2 leek, cut into thin strips*

*1/2 red pepper
2 tablespoons dry
  vermouth or sherry
2 tablespoons table cream
  (optional)
1 tablespoon butter
salt and pepper to taste*

Serves 2
Preparation time:
10 minutes
Cooking time:
About 20 minutes
Freezing:
Not recommended

1. Slit the chicken breasts nearly in half horizontally. Insert the ham and cheese, close up and re-form.
2. Blanch the leek strips in boiling water for 1 minute; drain well. Set aside a few strips.
3. Place the remaining leek strips on 2 sheets of greased waxed paper and arrange the chicken on top.
4. Cut out 6 hearts from the pepper, using a cutter if you have one. Place on top of the chicken and form kisses, i.e. xxx, with the reserved leeks.
5. Season with salt and pepper, pour over the vermouth or sherry and cream, if using, and dot with the butter. Fold the paper over the chicken and twist the ends to form 'crackers'. If you wish, make foil 'bows' and attach to each end.
6. Place on a baking sheet and cook in a preheated oven, 180°C/350°F, for about 20 minutes, until tender. Keep warm until required. Serve with buttered rice sprinkled with parsley, or pasto bows, and a tomato salad.

PINK PASSION CRUSH

*250 g (8 oz) strawberries
2 ripe passion fruit, halved
1 tablespoon fine sugar
  (optional)*

*3 tablespoons whipping
  cream
1 egg white*

Serves 2
Preparation time:
15 minutes, plus
chilling
Freezing:
Not recommended

1. Reserve 2 strawberries for decoration. Halve and mash the rest lightly—do not make too runny.
2. Scoop the passion fruit pulp into a small sieve and rub the juice through into the strawberries. Add the sugar if you wish.
3. Whip the cream and egg white separately until both are stiff, then fold lightly into the fruit mixture.
4. Pile into individual glass dishes and decorate with the reserved strawberries, halved. Chill until required. Serve with thin dessert biscuits.

SAVOURIES

SARDINE AND SESAME SEED ROLLS

These can be made up in advance and baked during the main course.

*4 slices whole grain bread,
  crusts removed*
*100 g (3.53 oz) can
  sardines in oil, drained
  and mashed*
1 green onion, chopped
1 tablespoon lemon juice
*1 teaspoon French
  mustard*
1 teaspoon chutney
3 anchovies, chopped
2 tablespoons butter, melted
2 teaspoons sesame seeds
pepper to taste

Serves 4
Preparation time:
15 minutes
Cooking time:
15 minutes
Freezing:
Not recommended

1. Roll the bread with a rolling pin until pliable.
2. Mix the sardines, green onion, lemon juice, mustard, chutney, anchovies and pepper together.
3. Spread on the bread, roll up firmly and cut each roll in half; secure with a wooden cocktail stick if necessary.
4. Brush with the butter, sprinkle with the sesame seeds and bake in a preheated oven, 200°C/400°F, for 15 minutes. Serve hot.

BACON AND PARMESAN ROLLS

Make these ahead and bake during the main course.

*4 slices whole grain bread,
  crusts removed*
*3 tablespoons butter,
  softened*
*40 g (1½ oz) Parmesan
  cheese, grated*
*few drops Worcestershire
  sauce*
4 bacon slices, halved
pepper to taste

Serves 4
Preparation time:
10 minutes
Cooking time:
15 minutes
Freezing:
Not recommended

1. Roll the bread with a rolling pin until pliable.
2. Mix a third of the butter with two thirds of the cheese, the Worcestershire sauce and pepper.
3. Spread on the bread and lay 2 half bacon slices on top. Roll up firmly and cut in half; secure with wooden cocktail sticks if necessary.
4. Spread the tops with the remaining butter and sprinkle with the remaining cheese. Bake in a preheated oven, 200°C/400°F, for 15 minutes. Serve hot.

SCOTCH WOODCOCK

This has to be freshly cooked but the toast can be prepared beforehand.

4 slices bread, crusts removed, toasted
¼ cup butter
anchovy paste, to spread
4–6 eggs, beaten

salt, pepper and ground mace to taste
TO GARNISH:
4 anchovy fillets, halved lengthways
8 large capers, or chopped parsley

1. Spread the toast sparingly with some of the butter and a little anchovy paste. Cut in half lengthways and sandwich together. Place on 4 small warmed plates.
2. Melt the remaining butter in a small pan and scramble the eggs. Season with pepper, mace, and a little salt.
3. Pile on the toast and garnish with the anchovies in a cross and the capers or parsley. Serve immediately.

Serves 4
Preparation time: 10 minutes
Cooking time: 10 minutes
Freezing: Not recommended

ICED CHEESE

250 g (8 oz) just ripe
    Camembert, Brie or
    Lymeswold cheese
12 radishes with stalks
small bunch of black
    grapes

4 small watercress sprigs
TO SERVE:
water biscuits, warmed
crushed ice

Serves 4
Preparation time:
10 minutes
Freezing:
Not recommended

1. Line 4 freezerproof side plates with a bed of crushed ice and place in the freezer until required.
2. Cut the cheese into 4 slices and arrange on the ice about 10 minutes before serving.
3. Garnish the cheese with the remaining ingredients. Serve with the warm water biscuits, and butter if you wish.

BROILED FETA CHEESE ON RYE

4 slices rye bread with
    caraway, toasted and
    buttered lightly
150 g (5 oz) Feta cheese,
    cut into 8 slices

1 tablespoon each chopped
    dill and mint
1/2 small cucumber, cut
    into sticks, to serve

Serves 4
Preparation time:
3–5 minutes
Cooking time:
10 minutes
Freezing:
Not recommended

1. Cut the toast in half lengthways. Top with the cheese and return to the broiler for 3–5 minutes, until golden.
2. Sprinkle with the herbs and serve immediately, accompanied by the cucumber.

STILTON AND WATERCRESS WAFERS

These can be made up an hour or so before the meal.

50 g (2 oz) blue Stilton
    cheese, derinded
1 tablespoon butter,
    softened
1/2 bunch watercress, leaves
    only, chopped

1 green onion, chopped
12 small water biscuits
TO GARNISH:
6 black olives, stoned and
    halved, or 3 cherry
    tomatoes, sliced

Serves 4–6
Preparation time:
15 minutes
Freezing:
Not recommended

1. Mash the Stilton and butter together until smooth, then mix in the watercress and green onion.
2. Spread on the biscuits, swirling attractively.
3. Garnish with the olives or tomatoes to serve.

DEVILLED NUTS

For after-meal nibbling. Prepare ahead and heat after the main course.

1 tablespoon butter
175 g (6 oz) whole
   blanched almonds or
   unsalted cashews, or a
   mixture of both

good pinch of garlic salt
¼ teaspoon cayenne
   pepper
fine sea salt or crushed
   rock salt to sprinkle

1. Melt the butter in a pan and allow to go light brown. Immediately remove from the heat and pour over the nuts. Add the garlic salt and cayenne and mix well.
2. Spread on a baking sheet and bake in a preheated oven, 200°C/400°F, for 15 minutes, shaking the nuts occasionally. Drain on kitchen paper.
3. Sprinkle with sea salt or rock salt and serve hot.

Serves 4
Preparation time:
5 minutes
Cooking time:
15 minutes
Freezing:
Not recommended

ACCOMPANIMENTS

PEAS WITH LETTUCE

150 ml (²/₃ cup) light stock
1 Romaine lettuce, sliced
1 onion, sliced

500 g (1 lb) frozen peas
1 tablespoon chopped mint
salt and pepper to taste

Serves 4–6
Preparation time:
10 minutes
Cooking time:
8 minutes
Freezing:
Not recommended

1. Place the stock in a large pan, add the lettuce and onion, cover and cook for 5 minutes.
2. Add the peas and mint and cook for 3 minutes. Season with salt and pepper and serve immediately.

CABBAGE WITH LEMON AND CARAWAY

1 small Chinese cabbage or
*   medium Savoy,*
*   shredded*
3 tablespoons butter

2 teaspoons caraway seeds
juice of 1 lemon
salt and pepper to taste

Serves 4–6
Preparation time:
5 minutes
Cooking time:
About 5 minutes
Freezing:
Not recommended

1. Boil or steam the cabbage for 3–5 minutes until just tender; drain.
2. Melt the butter in a small pan, add the caraway seeds and fry lightly for 1 minute. Add the lemon juice.
3. Toss into the cabbage, add salt and pepper and serve.

GREEN BEANS IN TOMATO CONCASSE

Any type of green bean is suitable for this dish. Top and tail, and string if necessary.

500 g (1 lb) green beans
2 tablespoons olive oil
1 small onion, chopped
4 tablespoons chopped
*   coriander leaves*

500 g (1 lb) tomatoes,
*   skinned, seeded and*
*   chopped*
salt and pepper to taste

Serves 4
Preparation time:
20 minutes
Cooking time:
6–9 minutes
Freezing:
Not recommended

1. Boil the beans in salted water for 5–8 minutes, according to taste; drain.
2. Meanwhile, heat the oil in a pan, add the onion and sauté for 5 minutes. Add the coriander and cook for 1 minute. Stir in the tomatoes and cook for 1 minute.
3. Toss into the beans, add salt and pepper and serve hot.

CARROTS SWEET AND SOUR

500 g (1 lb) carrots, cut
   into julienne strips
5 green onions, shredded
2 thyme sprigs
1 teaspoon chopped fresh
   root ginger
½ teaspoon salt

2 tablespoons light brown
   soft sugar
1 tablespoon lemon or
   lime juice
pepper to taste
chopped parsley to serve

Serves 4–6
Preparation time:
10 minutes
Cooking time:
10–15 minutes
Freezing:
Recommended

1. Place all the ingredients in a pan, add enough water just to cover and simmer, uncovered, for 10–15 minutes, until all the liquid has evaporated.
2. Garnish with parsley to serve.

POTATOES BOULANGÈRE

1 kg (2 lb) potatoes, sliced
   thinly
1 large onion, sliced thinly
600 ml (2½ cups) light stock

2 tablespoons butter, melted
salt, pepper and grated
   nutmeg to taste

Serves 6
Preparation time:
20 minutes
Cooking time:
About 1½ hours
Freezing:
Not recommended

1. Layer the potato and onion slices in a shallow casserole, seasoning the layers well with salt, pepper and nutmeg. Finish with potato slices.
2. Pour in the stock and brush potatoes with the butter. Cook in a preheated oven, 180°C/350°F, for about 1½ hours, until cooked and crisp on top. Serve hot.

CREAMED SPROUTS

1 kg (2 lb) Brussels sprouts
113 g (4 oz) carton
   cottage cheese
salt, pepper and grated
   nutmeg to taste

2 tablespoons slivered
   almonds, toasted, to
   serve

Serves 6
Preparation time:
10 minutes
Cooking time:
About 10 minutes
Freezing:
Not recommended

1. Boil the sprouts in salted water for about 10 minutes, until just tender. Drain, reserving a little water.
2. Place half of the sprouts and cheese in a food processor or blender and work until smooth. Transfer to a warmed serving dish. Repeat with remaining sprouts and cheese.
3. Add a little of the reserved cooking liquid if the purée is too dry. Season with salt, pepper and nutmeg.
4. Sprinkle with the almonds to serve.

BABY RÖSTI

500 g (1 lb) small potatoes,
    halved
175 g (6 oz) parsnips or
    turnips, cut into 5 cm
    (2 inch) pieces
3 green onions, sliced
    thinly

1 clove garlic, crushed
2 tablespoons butter
3 tablespoons oil
salt, pepper and ground
    mace to taste

Makes about 6
Preparation time:
15 minutes
Cooking time:
About 20 minutes
Freezing:
Recommended

1. Cook the potato and parsnip or turnip in boiling salted water for 8 minutes. Leave to cool, then grate coarsely into a bowl. Add the green onion, garlic, and salt, pepper and mace and mix well.
2. Heat half of the butter and oil in a heavy-based frying pan and add half of the potato mixture. Using a 7.5 cm (3 inch) metal scone cutter, press into 3 patties in the pan; do not cook with the cutter in position.
3. Cook for about 5 minutes, until browned, then turn and cook the other side for about 5 minutes. Keep warm, uncovered, in a low oven while cooking the remaining mixture. Serve hot.

BROWN RICE WITH BROCCOLI, CELERY AND NUTS

1 cup brown rice
750 ml (3 cups) light stock
1 tablespoon butter
250 g (8 oz) broccoli
    florets
3 tablespoons sunflower
    oil
1 clove garlic, crushed
2 celery sticks, sliced
    diagonally

4 green onions, sliced
    diagonally
2 tablespoons soy sauce or
    mushroom ketchup
salt and pepper to taste
1/4 cup hazelnuts or
    slivered almonds,
    toasted, to garnish
    (optional)

Serves 4
Preparation time:
15 minutes
Cooking time:
30 minutes
Freezing:
Recommended

1. Place the rice and stock in a pan, cover and simmer gently for 30 minutes. Add the butter.
2. Meanwhile, break the broccoli into small pieces and slice the stalks if necessary.
3. Towards the end of the rice cooking time, heat the oil and garlic in a pan, add the vegetables and stir-fry for about 5 minutes. Add the soy sauce or ketchup, and salt and pepper.
4. Stir into the rice and garnish with the nuts, if you wish.

VEGETABLE PURÉES

Not an idea for coping with soggy or stale vegetables, but a delicious way of serving fresh ones. You will need a food processor, blender or large mouli.

Boil or steam the vegetable as usual, seasoned or unseasoned, until just tender; do not overcook or the purée will be runny. Drain very well, then purée in a food processor or blender or rub through a mouli until smooth, but still thick enough to hold its shape. Add about 3 tablespoons cream, yogurt, soft butter or cooking water for every 500 g (1 lb) vegetables. Season with salt and pepper and add a flavouring if you wish. The following suggestions go well together:

- Brussels sprouts with grated nutmeg or ground mace
- Carrots with chopped thyme, ground ginger or ground coriander
- Parsnips with mild curry powder and pine nuts
- Peas with chopped mint
- Turnips with grated orange rind
- Beet with horseradish relish
- Cauliflower with chopped tarragon and lemon juice

An attractive serving idea is to make up two contrasting colour purées and pipe them in alternate stripes on a serving platter. Sprinkle with chopped herbs or toasted almonds, pine nuts or sesame seeds, if you wish.

Purées can be made ahead and reheated when required.

SIDE SALADS

Salads are a good dinner accompaniment for the busy cook-hostess—they can be prepared up to 24 hours ahead and kept bagged up and chilled. Do not dress leafy vegetables until ready to serve. Sliced tomatoes, grated raw carrots, and Waldorf-type salads can be dressed about 2 hours beforehand. Cold potato, rice and pasta salads should be tossed with vinaigrette while still hot, then mixed with other ingredients when cold.

Many new varieties of green salad vegetables are now available for much of the year and make an attractive feature on the table. Try and mix about three leafy vegetables, such as endive (frisé), shredded Romaine lettuce, radicchio, young spinach, mâche (lambs' lettuce) and oakleaf lettuce. Add thinly sliced cucumber, chicory or celery and sprinkle with chopped herbs. Pour over a well flavoured vinaigrette or thin pouring cream dressing just before serving and toss at the table. Scatter some toasted almonds on top to give a tasty crunch.

Adventurous gardeners may like to grow sorrel, purslane or rocket, or allow some dandelion plants to thrive and pick the young leaves to add to salads. Nasturtium leaves and flowers add a peppery flavour. Other leafy salad herbs include borage, salad burnet and Good King Henry.

An attractive presentation for all leafy or mixed salads is to layer them in a glass bowl. Put springy leaf vegetables at the base, then add the heavier ingredients. Finish with a layer of sliced tomato, radish or carrot, or some edible flowers like nasturtium or borage.

INDEX

Photography by: Andy Seymour
Designed by: Sue Storey
Home economist: Carole Handslip
Stylist: Penny Legg
Illustration by: Linda Smith
Typeset by Rowland Phototypesetting Limited